U.S. Marines Coloring Book

Oorah! American Soldiers In Military Action &
Combat Scenes – Patriotic Coloring

Rachel Mintz
Guest Illustrator: 'Sidharth Ojha

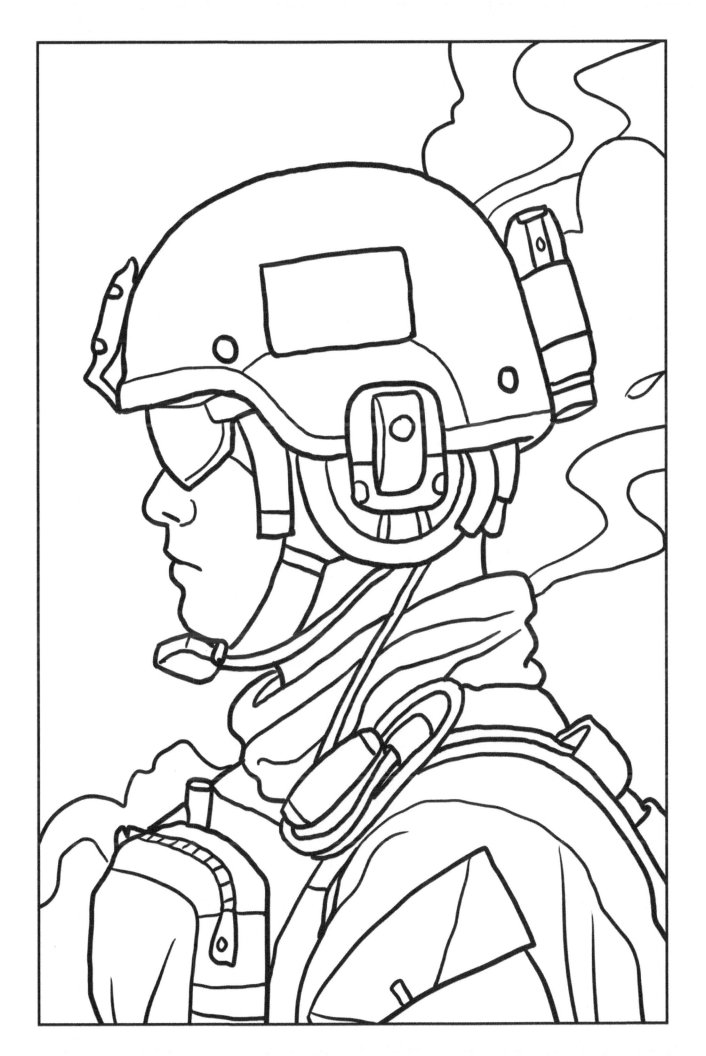

Thank you for coloring with us, we hope you had fun, please rate and review us, it would be awesome! Thanks

Rachel Mintz

SPECIAL
FORCES
COLORING BOOK
FOR KIDS AGES 8+

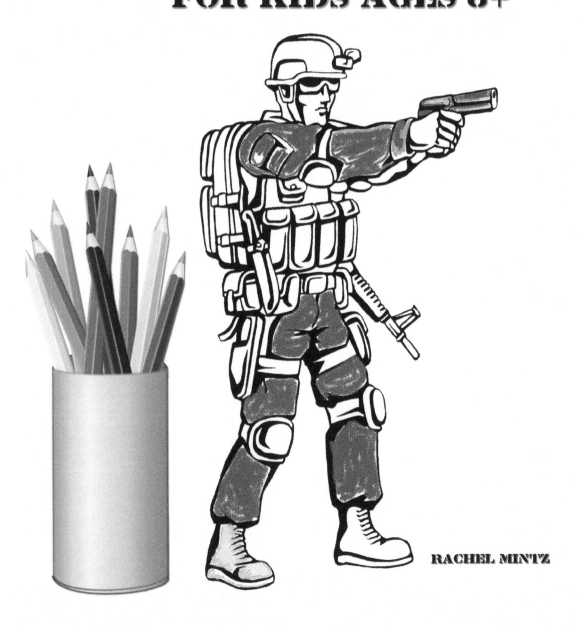

RACHEL MINTZ

Enjoy More Coloring Books By: *Rachel Mintz*

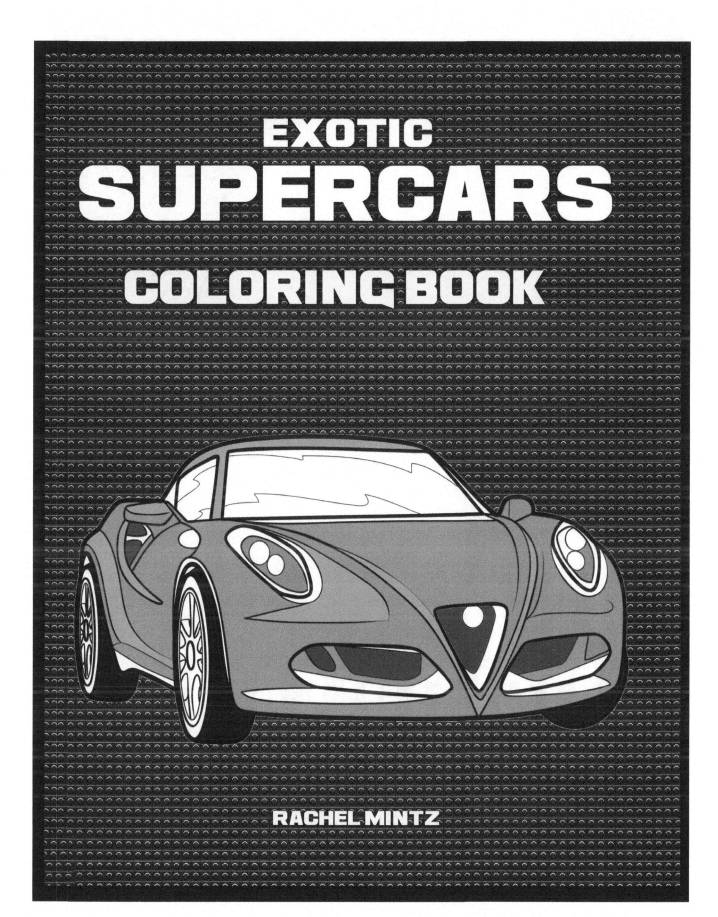

U.S.A

RACHEL MINTZ

PATRIOTIC EAGLES

BLACK PAGES COLORING BOOK

Enjoy More Coloring Books By: *Rachel Mintz*

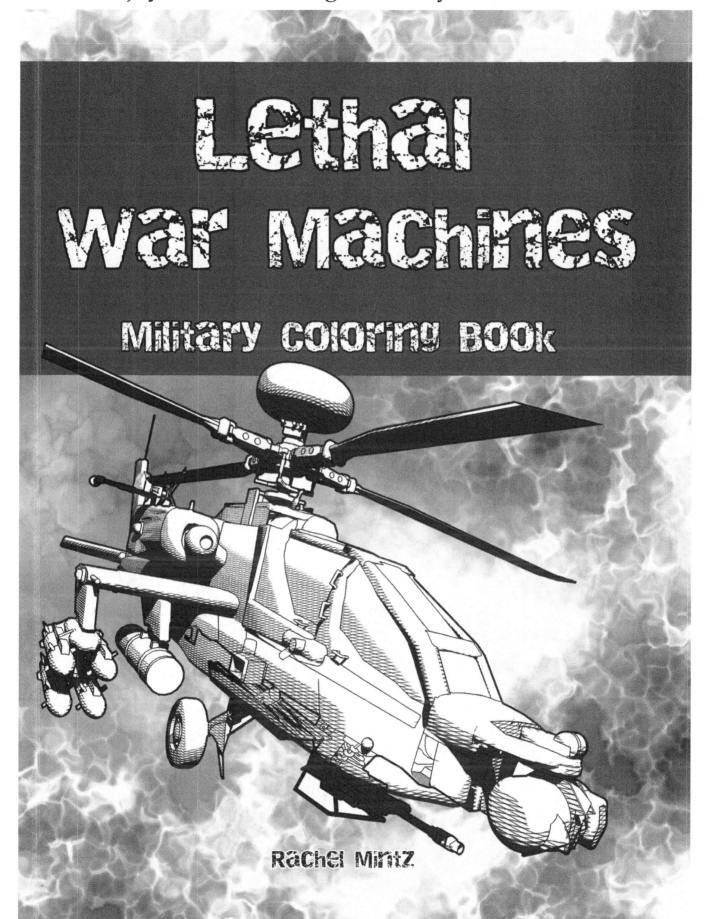

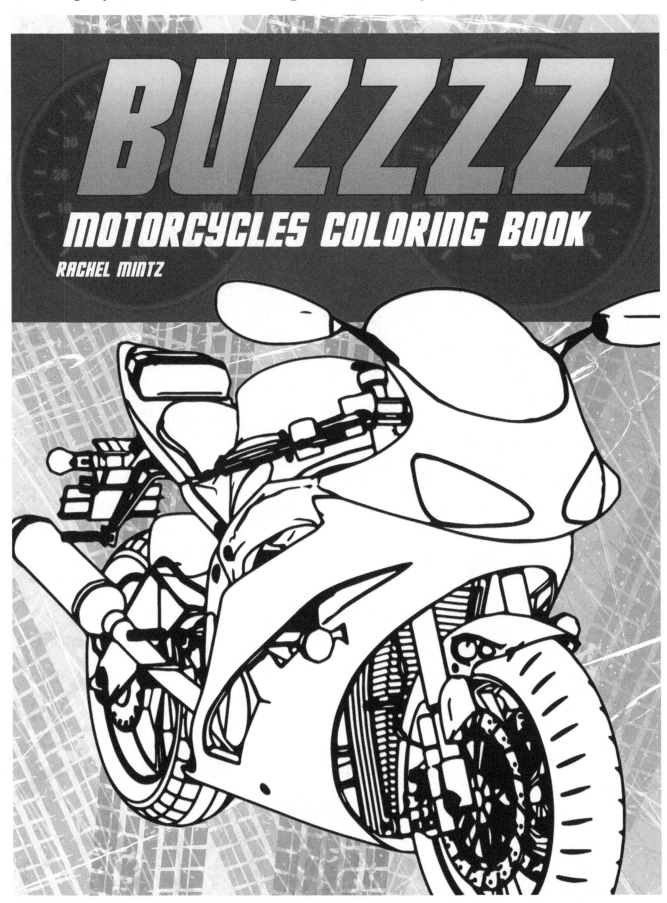

Thank you for coloring with us
Please take a moment to rate & review

Made in the USA
Coppell, TX
06 December 2021